Paddington's
123

by Michael Bond

Illustrated by John Lobban

Devised by Carol Watson

COLLINS

William Collins Sons & Co Ltd
London · Glasgow · Sydney · Auckland
Toronto · Johannesburg

First published 1990
© Michael Bond 1990
© illustrations Wm Collins Sons & Co Ltd 1990

A CIP catalogue record for this book is available from the British Library

ISBN 0 00 185118 7

Printed and bound in Portugal by Resopal.
This book is set in Century Schoolbook.

1

One Paddington Bear

2

two boots

3

three suitcases

4

four toggles

5

five
knickerbocker
glories

6

six hats

7

seven mugs

8

eight candles

9

nine postcards

10

ten buckets

11

eleven spades

12

twelve flags

13

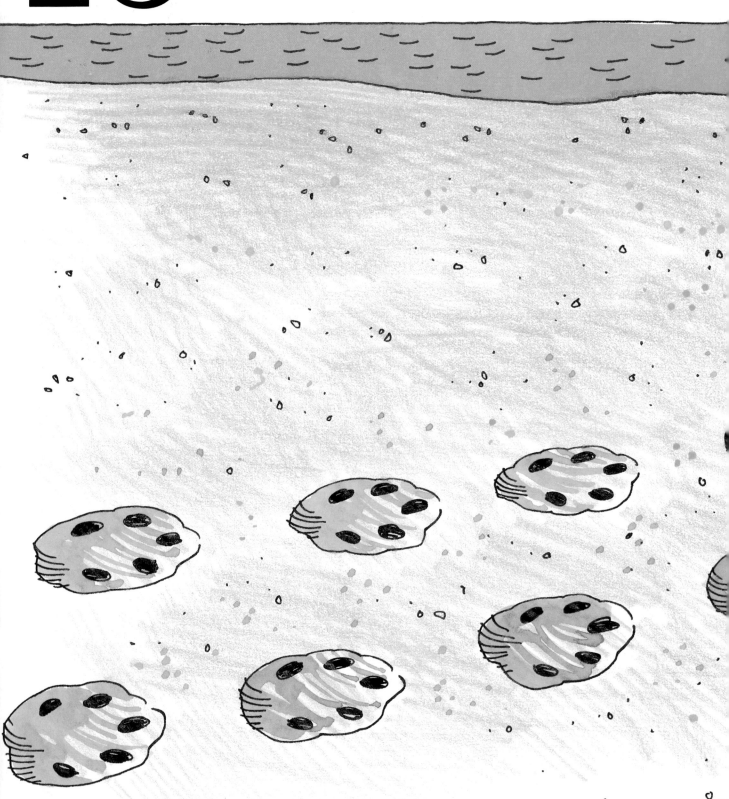

thirteen pawprints

14

fourteen balloons

15

fifteen jars of
marmalade

16

sixteen crayons

17

seventeen jam tarts

eighteen stars

19

nineteen fish

twenty marmalade sandwiches

Now there are only 19 sandwiches left! Can you find them hidden in this picture?

1
2
3
4
5
6
7
8
9
10
11
12
13
14
15
16
17
18
19
20

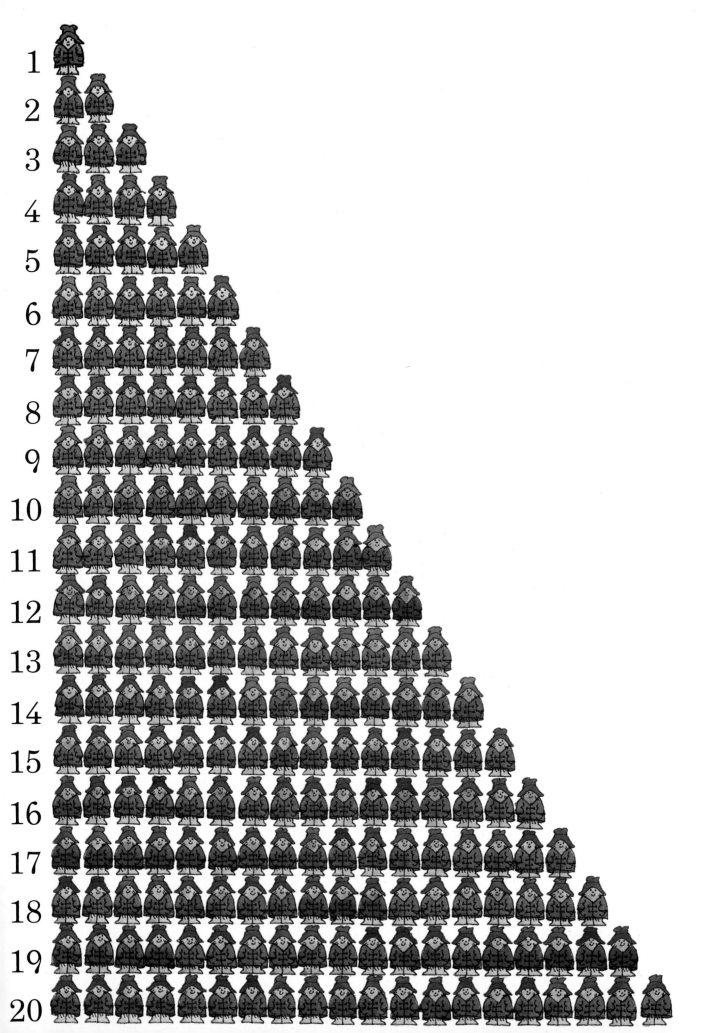